JEWS OF THE WILD WEST
A MULTICULTURAL TRUE STORY

WRITTEN AND ILLUSTRATED BY KAY MILLER

INTEREST LEVEL
AGES 8 TO 108

ISBN 978-0-615-55388-7

LIBRARY OF CONGRESS CONTROL NUMBER: 2012900839

DEDICATED TO THE STAABS AND ILFELDS OF NEW MEXICO

Teenage brothers Abraham and Zadock Staab heard the stories of gold, trade and wealth in America. They were Jewish and living in Germany. The tales sounded a lot more exciting than life in their crowded Jewish neighborhood. Germans considered Jews to be outsiders and foreigners for as long as anyone could remember. Jews were treated as if they didn't belong there. Even though recent laws declared Jews to be equal citizens the old attitudes toward Jews were slow to go away. The brothers were at risk of being drafted into the army and forced into combat. They did not want to fight for Germany so they left in 1854 hoping for a better future.

Abraham and Zadoc endured two weeks on a ship across the stormy Atlantic Ocean. The ship rocked from side to side. Waves beat the ship violently at times. The unpredictable motion made the brothers nauseous. Arriving in Norfolk, Virginia was a huge relief. The morning sun sprinkled the bay with golden glitter. Leafy green trees lined the outer areas. Abraham and Zadoc worked for relatives there for one dollar a week.

After four years, the brothers moved to Santa Fe, New Mexico. The land was very different, with rose-colored soil surrounded by mountains. It really was the Wild West. There were battles between settlers and Native Americans. Thieves roamed on horseback. Lawmen were challenged to keep the peace and prevent jailbreaks.

Despite all that, there were more opportunities to make a good living. The brothers worked for their relatives the Spiegelbergs, who were merchants. In 1859, Zadok and Abraham were able to open their own small store. They named it Z. Staab and Brother. It was a general store that sold practical items including underwear, medicine and food. Soon after, they decided that one brother needed to be in New York City to purchase goods and get government contracts. Zadok left for New York. Both young men continued to work hard in separate cities.

Twelve years later the Staab brothers were running the store and a large warehouse. They also had a factory in New York. The brothers made and sold a huge variety of items, everything from party dresses to shovels. In 1881 it was written in the newspaper, The New Mexican, that the Staabs did nearly a million dollars worth of business. They were doing a lot better than when they started out in Virginia! Their business area included New Mexico, west Texas, eastern Arizona, San Francisco and old Mexico, especially Ciudad Chihuahua. The business provided jobs for many people. The Staab brothers' determination and years of labor allowed their American dream to come true.

Abraham was a friend of Archbishop Jean-Baptiste Lamy, the leader of the Catholics in Santa Fe. Born in France, Lamy was one of 11 children from a religious family. Many of his brothers and sisters became missionaries, priests and nuns. Lamy built the first school to teach English in Santa Fe in 1852.

He was overseeing the building of a new church, the Saint Francis Cathedral in 1869. It was spectacular and took 17 years to build. The archbishop borrowed a large amount of money for the construction from Abraham. Later it became clear that Lamy could not afford to repay the money. A generous Abraham tore up the loan note. He made the loan a gift. Archbishop Lamy had Hebrew letters written in stone above the entrance to the Cathedral. The letters spelled God. He also had a Jewish star placed over the side entrance. This was Lamy's way of saying thank you to Abraham. Abraham felt proud every time he saw the Hebrew and the star above the cathedral doorways. If you're in Santa Fe, you can go to see them too.

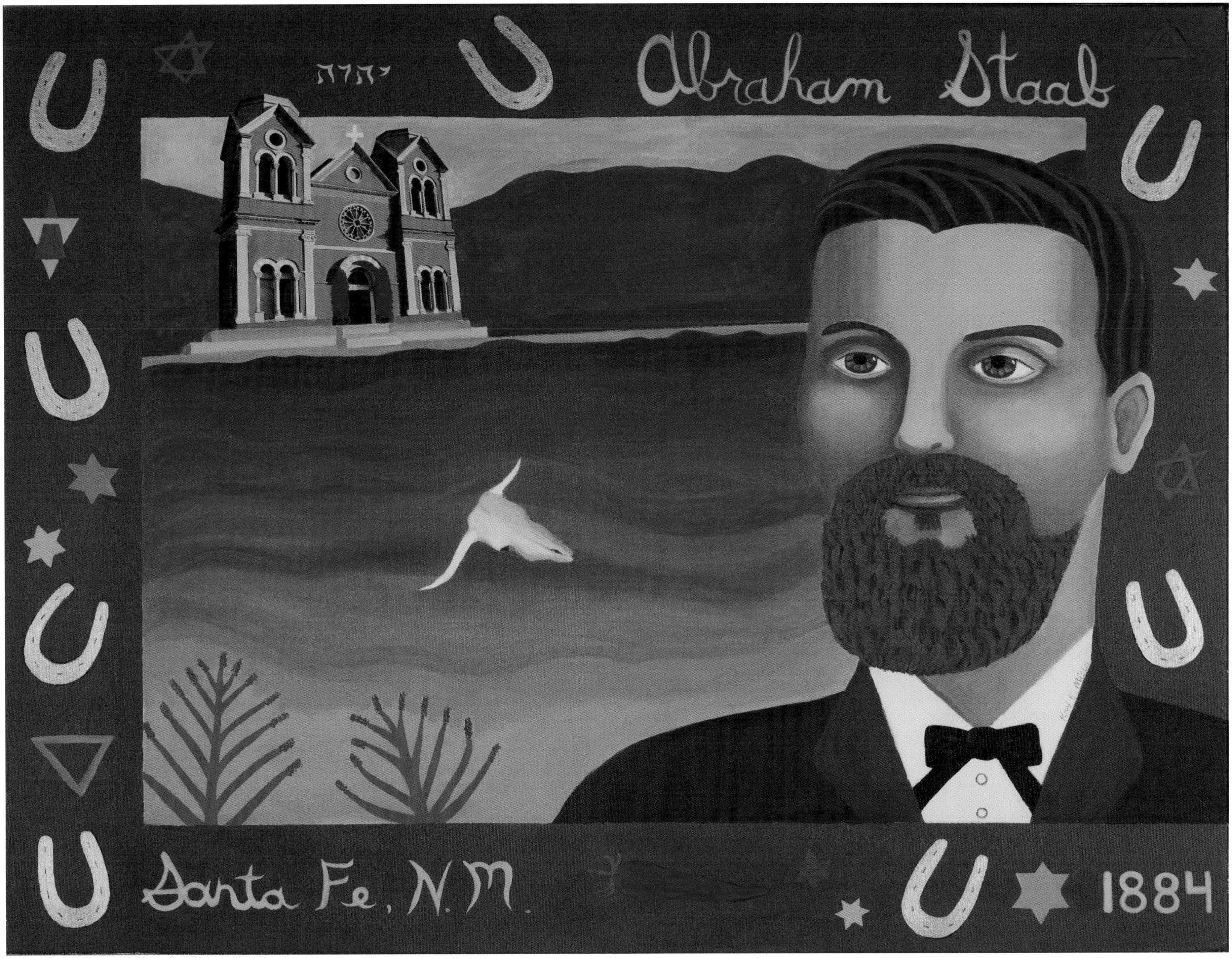
יהוה
Abraham Staab
Santa Fe, N.M.
1884

Abraham and his wife, Julia, had six children. Whenever Abraham played poker in the evening, the next morning at breakfast he would place a $20 gold coin on each child's plate. Abe hoped to convince Julia that he had won money the night before.

Abraham ran a bank for the community. His safe was used to store money. He also helped to bring the railroad to Santa Fe. Abraham was appreciated for his honesty. He was the first president of the Santa Fe Chamber of Commerce. He earned the wealth he sought with honor. You can visit Abraham and Julia's splendid Victorian house in Santa Fe at La Posada.

Julia Staab was not only a mom. She often hosted fancy parties at the mansion on Palace Avenue. Guests included President Rutherford B. Hayes, rabbis, governors, business people, Archbishop Lamy, members of the military and the community. Entertaining guests at her fabulous home was fun and interesting for Julia. She could afford to wear gorgeous gowns. You were considered lucky to receive an invitation to a Staab party.

Julia's life was not always so glamorous. Once when she was traveling by stagecoach with a Catholic nun named Sister Blandina, the women had a scary encounter. All of a sudden the bandit Billy the Kid and his gang were racing toward Julia and Blandina on horseback. The women were terrified that they would be robbed and maybe killed. When Billy got a little closer he recognized Sister Blandina. She had nursed him back to health after an injury. Because of Blandina's kindness in the past, Billy and his gang did not rob or harm the women. Blandina and Julia thanked God for keeping them safe.

After the birth of Julia's youngest child, tragedy visited the family. The child died in a third-floor fire. Julia became depressed and ill. Her hair turned white from the sorrow and stress. It was very hard for her to cope with the loss of a child. She remained ill until she died about 15 years later at the age of 52. Currently there are many stories about her ghost haunting the Palace Avenue house. You can take the ghost tour there if you dare.

Julia Staab 1884

Santa Fe, N.M.

Julia's daughter, Bertha, grew up to be an adventurous woman. She went with Governor Hagerman and a group of friends to the Hopi tribe's snake dances. They traveled six days by horse and wagon to get to the Hopi pueblo. The name Hopi means peaceful people.

The Hopi made colorful clothing with woven designs which they wore at the ceremony. Snakes were considered part of the earth and the water of springs and lakes. The snake dance was the acting out of a prayer for rain. Hopi men handled live rattlesnakes in the ceremony! Imagine the excitement of watching the dancers handle the poisonous snakes.

Bertha was kind and cared about kids. She worked to help orphans and unwanted children for 30 years. Bertha and her husband, Max, had three children of their own whom they loved very much.

Charles Ilfeld, a handsome 18-year-old Jew, left Germany and headed for New Mexico in 1865. Charles hoped for adventure and riches in America. After his ship landed in New York City, there was a train ride across many states. Next was a trip on a ferry. Finally, a three-month, bumpy ox wagon ride landed Charles Ilfeld in Santa Fe.

Charles' older brother, Herman, was already living in Santa Fe and ran a business there. Herman made Charles his bookkeeper because of his math ability. Charles' job was to keep track of the purchase and sale of buffalos, pinion nuts, corn, wool, furs, chilies, eggs, sheep and Native American blankets and rugs. He kept track of the amounts, prices and totals of the money paid and received.

Once when Charles was low on money, he borrowed $5,000 in gold from a man of Spanish descent. There was nothing in writing about paying back the money because the man trusted Charles. Not only was the money paid back, but interest on the loan was paid as well. Because Charles was honest and responsible he earned the Spanish nickname Tio Carlos which means Uncle Charlie, a respected title.

After several years Charles saved enough money to open his own store. Charles packed his merchandise on the backs of 75 burros and led the herd to Las Vegas, New Mexico. His store there carried many everyday items such as pots and pans, kerosene lamps, food and blankets. The store had one cash register that sat on a counter top. The first year Charles slept on the floor under the counter to protect his shop from thieves. By 1882, Charles had enough money to build a large building on the plaza. He moved his store there. People called his department store Ilfeld's on the Plaza.

The "Ilfeld's on the Plaza" building still exists today as part of the Plaza Hotel. There are antiques from Charles' store on display at the hotel. There is also an auditorium building in Las Vegas that Charles gave to the local school.

Charles "Tio Carlos" Ilfeld

Las Vegas, N.M.   1890

Charles met a freed slave named Montgomery Bell at the Montezuma Hotel in Las Vegas. Charles liked Montgomery's attentiveness and intelligence. Montgomery's job was managing the stables at the hotel. African Americans had been treated terribly in the American south. Charles wanted Montgomery to have a better life. He made Montgomery an agent for the Charles Ilfeld Company.

Eventually Montgomery earned enough pay to start his own cattle and sheep business. Montgomery built one of the first two-story houses in Las Vegas for his family. The opportunity of a good job plus hard work brought Montgomery and his family a comfortable life. Charles found adventure in New Mexico. He earned riches and the respect of his community.

In 1892, Charles' 16-year-old nephew Ludwig Ilfeld arrived in Las Vegas. Ludwig had a lot of energy and many interests. Ludwig wore multiple hats in his lifetime. That means he had a lot of different jobs. He started out working for Uncle Charlie. Next, as a salesman for the Wolf-American Company, he sold bicycles around the world. Ludwig spoke fluent German, English, French, Yiddish and Spanish which helped him in his travels. When he returned to New Mexico, he wore yet another hat: that of fire chief of East Las Vegas. He held that position for 53 years. Ludwig owned a hardware store in town. He started a rodeo and even acted in a cowboy movie called "The Rattlesnake."

Ludwig married a woman named Minnie and they had four children. There were three boys, Carl, Max and Fred. Their daughter's name was Florence. Ludwig enjoyed taking his family fishing, camping and horseback riding.

Ludwig loved horses and so did his pal, Teddy Roosevelt. Ludwig lent his horse Maude to Teddy to ride in the Rough Riders Parade which Ludwig organized in Las Vegas, New Mexico. The Rough Riders were volunteer soldiers who rode horses into battle in the Spanish American War. When Teddy was elected president of the United States, he invited Ludwig to his inauguration. Ludwig rode a horse in the inauguration parade.

Montefiore was the first synagogue of New Mexico, in Las Vegas. There was a time when the synagogue had only a part-time rabbi. When the rabbi was not available, Ludwig supervised at the bar mitzvahs and performed the weddings and funerals. He served his country as a member of the National Guard. He also raised money for several charities including the Red Cross. You could say that Ludwig was a very busy fellow.

Ludwig Ilfeld   Teddy Roosevelt

Las Vegas NM   1914

Louis Ilfeld, Charles' brother, married Anna Staab, a daughter of Abraham and Julia. The Staab and Ilfeld families became one big extended family.

When the Ilfelds went to Santa Fe to visit the Staabs, they would bring their own cow. The Ilfelds thought their cow's milk tasted better than the milk from the Staabs' cow!

an Ilfeld cow

1915   Santa Fe, N.M.

Robert Nordhaus was born in Las Vegas, New Mexico in 1909. He was the son of Abraham Staab's daughter, Bertha and of Max Nordhaus. Max was Charles Ilfeld's brother-in-law. When Robert was a little boy, he would slide down the banister of the main staircase of his Grandpa Abraham's house. When he grew up, he was athletic. He joined the 10th Mountain Division of the army in 1942. Robert was trained to ski, rock climb and snowshoe in combat. He used these skills to fight the Nazis in the mountains of Europe during World War II.

Robert Nordhaus

Santa Fe, N.M. 1915

Robert was a lawyer in Albuquerque, New Mexico during peace time. His law office specialized in Native American rights. Robert argued on behalf of the Jicarilla Apaches at the U.S. Supreme Court, the most powerful court in America.

The Apaches wanted to tax oil companies that were drilling on their land. The lawyer representing the oil companies claimed that the land did not belong to the Apaches.

Robert prepared for the case by studying ancient Apache tipi rings. Circles of stone were placed around tipis to hold the edges down. The circles remained long after the tipis were gone. After settlers introduced axes to the Apaches the stones were replaced with wooden pegs.

Thurgood Marshall, the first African American Supreme Court Justice, wrote the majority opinion of the court. The court's decision was in favor of the Apaches. Robert proved that the land belonged to the tribe. The Apaches were able to tax the oil companies. They used the tax money to start their own oil company. It was the first Native American-owned oil company in America. The tribe showed their appreciation by making Robert an honorary Jicarilla Apache. Robert wrote a book about the court case called "Tipi Rings - A Chronicle of the Jicarilla Apache Land Claim."

Robert had a friend and business partner named Ben Abruzzo. Together, they started the Sandia Peak Ski Slopes in 1960. While visiting Europe, Robert rode a tram and that made him want a tram ride at Sandia Slopes. The tramway was built 4,000 feet up Sandia Mountain near Albuquerque. It is the longest passenger tramway in the world. More than 9 million people have ridden the tram at Sandia Mountain and you can too!

Robert turned his interests in skiing, law and helping others into his life's work. Because he was able to work at what he enjoyed, he had a happy life. He lived to be 97 years old.

The Staab and Ilfeld families found opportunity in New Mexico. Because of their honesty, generosity and hard work, they helped make New Mexico a better place to live, work and play.

About The Author

Kay Miller is a descendent of the Staab and Ilfeld families. Her grandmother Ruth Ilfeld was raised in Albuquerque. Kay grew up in Cincinnati. Horseback riding lessons at Winton Woods was one of her favorite childhood activities.

Kay is a retired New York City public school teacher. She researched her family history with documents, books on Jewish settlers of the Wild West, interviews of relatives and the internet. Her home is in New Jersey where she lives with her husband and dog Trixie.